Why should we sit quietly ?

The place of teenagers in today's Church

Justyn **Evans**

First published in 1999 by
KEVIN MAYHEW LTD
Buxhall
Stowmarket
Suffolk IP14 3DJ

0 1 2 3 4 5 6 7 8 9

ISBN 1 84003 391 6
Catalogue No 1500286

Edited by Elisabeth Bates
Cover designed by Jonathan Stroulger
Illustrated by Fred Chevalier
Typesetting by Richard Weaver
Printed and bound in Great Britain

Contents

Introduction

Think back, if you can, to that period of seven years of change in your life, the teenage years. For some, it was just a few years ago; for others, several decades. Even if you can remember what it was like to be a teenager then, it doesn't necessarily mean you know what it's like to be one now. As the years have changed, so has society. It's not just technology that has revolutionised our lives, social attitudes have been relaxed, and a whole lot more besides. Being a Christian teenager today is not like it was a few decades ago – and it's still not easy. And I should know: I am a one. And what's more, I've been one for the last few years.

If you're a youth leader or a pastor, a teacher or a parent, or any other adult, then this book is written for you. I wrote it to tell others what it's like to be a Christian teenager today, and I hope having read it, you will feel you know a little bit more about today's teenagers. Of course, I can't claim to speak for all teenagers! I can only speak from my own experiences and observations.

So, why should we (teenagers) sit quietly? I've thought a lot about this question, and this book is my response to it. The only answer I can give is that we shouldn't have to. This book contains the thoughts and views of one Christian teenager who doesn't want to sit quietly – me! I'm no one special, I'm just your average teenager. Everyone's got their own views, and these are some of mine . . .

WHY SHOULD THE DEVIL HAVE ALL THE GOOD MUSIC ???

. . . You wave the Bible and you scream and you shout
but you don't have a clue what you're talkin' about.

You been goin' through the Churches like a Nazi for Truth
sayin' Christian rock music is destroyin' the youth,
slanderin' your brothers that you don't even know,
ruinin' reputations every place that you go.

You call it devil music, say it's right from the pits,
scarin' parents everywhere right out of their wits,
they're goin' to your meetin's buyin' books and buyin' tapes,
but all you're sellin's legalism, guilt, and sour grapes.

I know you wouldn't use it for your Sunday mornin' service,
but that ain't no excuse to get so spiritually nervous,
I know you don't like it, but now listen my friend,
just 'cause you don't like it doesn't mean it's a sin! . . .

Don Francisco – *Freedom to move*

So why should the devil get to have all the good music? I don't think he should – after all it was God who created music, so I don't see why Christians can't have good music as well. Music is a powerful tool that can be used to aid worship, or simply to help relaxation. Music can unite or divide, it can break barriers or strengthen them, it has the power to heal or to hurt. It is a concoction of noises that somehow fit together, like the pieces in a puzzle, to form a tune. But everyone has their own individual preferences, their likes and dislikes; for instance, if you listened to some of my favourite songs, you might not even call them music! I guess it's a case of 'each to his own!'

Most teenagers have their own preferences and dislikes, and it's not only teenagers either, adults too, like to listen to music but prefer some styles to others. There are so many styles of music on the market today because everyone is different, everyone is unique. Whether it be classical, jazz, hip hop, rave, jungle, or garage (whatever next?) there is a style to suit every taste.

Music's part of our culture

Just as some people like garlic and others don't, or some like their curries hot and others prefer them mild, so everyone has their own tastes when it comes to music. The flavour of music that I like is almost certainly going to be different from the flavour of music that you like. I think that music is often a part of our personality, a part of our identity, a part of our culture. It is almost as if the music we listen to forms our character. Just as some people's personalities seem to clash at times, musical tastes can also clash.

The generation gap between young people and their parents is often widened by music. It seems that young people like a totally different kind of music from their parents. I think music plays a role in developing our identities, and it helps us to become individuals, so it's not surprising that our musical tastes are different from our parents'.

It's a generation thing

If you're an adult who doesn't like the music of today's young people (and sadly, if this is the case, then you're probably in the majority), try to think back to the kind of music that your parents liked when they were your age. Of course, when they were your age, you were probably a teenager yourself. Did they like the music that you listened to? I doubt they did, I should imagine they liked a different sort of music. It's just the same with the teenagers of today, we generally seem to like a different sort of music from you, our parents. Every generation seems to like a different sort of music, but can this go on for ever? I mean, there can't be many styles of music left to be discovered or invented, can there?

The big question is, did you like it when your parents didn't like the kind of music that you listened to? Did you like them shouting at you for playing it too loud? (or whatever you did with your music?) No, of course you didn't, and guess what? We don't either! So if you do keep criticising today's teenagers because of the music we listen to, then why not try to remember what it feels like to be criticised – remember, this music is part of our generation, and part of our culture – it's us. Criticise our music and you're basically criticising us, and that's not too nice. Not everyone is against today's music (don't look so startled, I'm not lying) some adults don't mind listening to it now and again. But they realise that life as a teenager is tough enough as it is and see that it's pointless to make it tougher. So why not let us listen to our music? – it's not as bad as you think.

Young people like contemporary music

Don Francisco sums it up in his song: there's nothing wrong with this kind of music just because it's not the sort that you'd use in your Sunday morning service. Just because it's got drums in it or a funky rhythm doesn't mean that it's the devil's. Towards the end of the song he says 'I know it isn't heavy ministry, the lyrics are light,' and that's so true. Much of today's CCM (Contemporary Christian Music) isn't full of deep theology, but neither are many things in life, and there's nothing wrong with relaxing a little now and again. There are many Christian bands who play good music; their lyrics are clean and they can be great to relax to, or enjoy.

Unfortunately there is lots of music that's not so good, but that's been the case for many years. What we should be looking at isn't the rhythm or the instruments used, but the words. What matters is the words and the motives behind them. If they're good, then does it matter what the music's like? If people like to listen to it and the words are getting through, then what's the harm?

The music of my generation, the music of today, seems to have got a bad name for itself. It seems to be associated far too much with drugs. I don't like these stereotypes – they seem unfair to me. Most people simply enjoy listening to the music and that's that, but then some people will go to raves, listen to music, dance and take drugs. Apart from breaking the law and getting themselves hospitalised, they're also giving modern music a bad name. When this happens everyone thinks it's because of the music, but in most cases it's not. There are a few singers who do convey the wrong message about drugs and who are not good role models, but there are many more who are good ones. Besides, as Christians we don't need to look to pop heroes or other music legends for role models – we have Jesus Christ himself as a role model. So what I'm basically saying is that there are always going to be bad role models and bad lyrics, but we must remember that there are also good ones and that modern music is not all bad – it's mostly good.

There are always two sides to every argument and I know many readers will be saying that I'm wrong and they're right – that modern music's not so good. I admit some of it may be bad, but as I've already said, lots of it is good. I'm not saying you have to like it, or even listen to it, just accept it!

Think about it

'. . . I know you don't like it, but now listen my friend
just 'cause you don't like it doesn't mean it's a sin! . . . '

Prayer

Lord Jesus,
  sometimes I don't mind listening to different styles of music,
  and other times I hate it.
  But help me to remember that in your eyes
  there's nothing wrong with most modern music.
  Amen.

WHAT! ANOTHER YOUTH MEETING?

THE CHURCH STILL HASN'T RECOVERED FROM THE LAST ONE!

Church diary – week beginning February 9th

Monday	- 10:00	Morning prayer meeting
Tuesday	- 09:30	Parent and Toddler group
	- 19:30	House groups
Wednesday	- 17:00	Banana Gang – children's club
Thursday	- 20:00	Prayer meeting
Saturday	- 07:00	Men's Breakfast – monthly meeting
	- 19:00	Valentine Special – youth meeting
Sunday	- 10:30	Morning Worship
	- 19:30	Evening Worship

Gertrude looked at her watch as she walked down the hallway of her bungalow. 'Good,' she murmured to herself, 'just gone a quarter past seven.' As she walked out the door she glanced in the mirror, checking her hair – it was fine. Ten minutes later she drove smoothly into the church car park and found a space. She turned off the engine, switched off the lights and got out of her car. She locked the car door and hurried through the car park towards the church, shivering in the night air. As she walked, she glanced around, wondering why she didn't recognise the other cars. Shrugging off that strange feeling she headed for the door of the church – it was open and light was pouring out.

As she got closer, she thought she could hear loud music; frowning, she tried to remember who was speaking. 'Must be some kind of illustration,' she thought, suddenly remembering the speaker: that youthful guy, James Johnson (who's actually more than thirty years old!). She walked into the porch, hung her coat up on a spare hook and opened the inner door. She walked in, expecting to see everyone sitting quietly in the pews, waiting for the service to begin – and listening to the strange music that James Johnson was playing.

Shocked and surprised, she stopped abruptly. Looking around she suddenly realised she hadn't come to a typical Sunday evening service – the place was crowded with young people wearing denim. The whole PA system was resounding to the noise of loud 'love' songs, and the drum beat was making the floor vibrate. One of the young people must have wired their CD player up to the PA. If that wasn't bad enough, on another table in the corner, bottles of pop stood open, half empty and there were biscuit crumbs on the carpet. The very carpet that she carefully vacuumed only a day or two before.

Shocked and unsure what to do, she hurriedly walked through the main hall and into the kitchen, wondering what on earth was happening. In the kitchen, used cups were piled high in the sink, but no one was about. Still puzzled, and wondering where the speaker had got to, she walked into another room and found a group playing table tennis and talking loudly. One of the young people, the one holding a broken table tennis bat in his hand, was even wearing a jumper advertising a popular brand of beer – despicable!

Trying to decide whether or not she should call the police,

Gertrude glanced around once more, finally recognising someone she knew. Sandra, the youth leader, walked up to her and calmly said 'Gertrude, this is a surprise! Welcome to our Youth Meeting, it's a Valentine Special.' As Gertrude began to realise that it was actually Saturday and not Sunday, her face turned the colour of beetroot, and after murmuring an excuse to Sandra, she hurried out. Feeling embarrassed that she had somehow got her days muddled, Gertrude drove home, wondering who would let such awful things happen in the church.

Do you know what happens at a youth meeting?

It probably isn't likely that you'd get your days mixed up, but just stop and think for a moment. How many people in your church actually know what goes on at youth meetings? If you were to walk in on one would you be scared and want to leave, like Gertrude did? Or would you be shocked and surprised? It's not surprising that so many people don't want the Christian youth of today to have youth activities, many people have no idea about what really happens, what really goes on.

I think Christian youth activities are a great idea, they help Christian teenagers to make friends with other Christians their own age. They are also a great opportunity for outreach and are often the ideal thing to bring non-Christian friends to. What better way is there to relax, than amongst supportive Christian friends? It's the perfect place to have fellowship with other Christians and learn more about God. At youth meetings there are often lots of fun activities, but more importantly there is an opportunity for the Bible to be discussed in a way that's relevant to the lives of young people, and in a way that young people can understand.

Young people want their own meetings

It's when we're teenagers that we develop most – so that's the time that activities are really needed. If there aren't things for teenagers at the church, you can guarantee that many teenagers will go elsewhere. Anyway, why shouldn't we have our own meetings/outreach evenings? The kids have their club, and the adults have loads of activities. Even the little toddlers have a group specially for them! So why not let us have some activities?

Think about it

In this day and age when there are so many alternative lifestyles, does your church cater for the needs of the youth? – not just the ones living on the street corners, but the ones who come to church on Sunday mornings. If it does, that's really great, but do you know what happens at these youth meetings? Do you pray regularly for the church's activities? If your church doesn't have youth meetings, is there anything you can do?

Prayer

Lord,
    I may not be a youth leader or a minister,
    and at times some teenagers even scare me,
    but I guess you have a role even for little me in your Church.
    Help me to fulfil that role
    and influence the lives of the young people I know.
    Amen.

... PRAISE HIM WITH **CRASHING** CYMBALS

Praise the Lord!
Praise God in his Temple;
praise him in his heaven.
Praise him for his strength;
praise him for his greatness.
Praise him with trumpet blasts;
praise him with harps and lyres.
Praise him with tambourines and dancing;
praise him with stringed instruments and flutes.
Praise him with loud cymbals;
praise him with crashing cymbals.
Let everything that breathes praise the Lord.

Praise the Lord!
Psalm 150 (NCV Anglicised Edition)

Praise and worship was noisy, even in Old Testament times

Wow! Imagine what it must have been like to praise God when the Psalms were written. This isn't the kind of stuff you sing with an old pipe organ, this is the business! Trumpets, harps, tambourines, flutes – the whole of the orchestra sang their praises to God. It wasn't quiet, either; they praised him with loud, crashing cymbals. This is incredible, just a few years ago those who dared to play drums in church were radicals. But it seems that the psalmist beat us to it, they had percussion back in David's day – and they used it! They praised God with loud and noisy instruments!

Imagine what it would have been like to be in the Temple courts praising the Lord. The noise of the instruments – loud, clear and beautiful. The dancers, the singers, all lifting up the name of the Lord in worship and praise. What would your average 20th century Christian say to this? Be honest – if you were there, you'd wonder what was going on!

Just suppose for a moment that time travel is possible, and that you have travelled back in time to David's day. As you enter the Temple courts you'd witness an amazing sight. A huge crowd of people lost in praise and admiration of an unseen being. The loud music hurts your ears and you can feel the ground vibrating as the people jump for joy – enthusiastically praising their Saviour. What would you do? The average Christian today would probably try to escape, scared that a riot might break out. So you look around and try to make for the exit; but crowds of people are pouring in through every doorway, eager to join the celebration, so there's no chance that you can get out. You stop for a moment and think, you remember your mobile phone and think you'll call the local police. You get it from your back-pack and try to turn it on, but it doesn't work. Puzzled, you try again. Suddenly you realise that electricity hasn't been discovered yet; worse still, no one dreamt up the idea of having a police force till long after the tenth century!

Or perhaps you realised what was going on, perhaps you recog-nised the noise of God's people singing his praises. Would you have joined in? Or would you have shied away and stood at the edge of the crowd watching?

I think that most of us would be shocked if we saw what it had been like in those Temple courts. Some adults often call those sort of people extremists or overly charismatic, and try to avoid them. But this Psalm makes it clear that there's nothing wrong with noisy worship. The trouble with praise and worship is that it's all too easy to sing the songs, singing along with the piano without ever really understanding the words. Without ever knowing why, without ever knowing the person you are singing to.

Worship and praise is not simply about singing and dancing, it is about expressing our adoration and love of God. The people in the Temple courts were doing just that, they were singing their thanks and praise, worshipping him from their hearts.

Young people like to worship with modern songs

What a contrast between then and now! Today we are more used to singing slow, nine verse hymns accompanied by the sound of an old organ, than to lively, joyful songs. What's happened? What's gone wrong? Many of today's youth prefer to praise and worship God by singing lively songs – this is us, our culture, our generation. But so many people don't like modern songs, they say it is wrong and irreverent to be noisy in God's presence. They tell us we should sing songs that are . . . dull!

Don't get me wrong, I haven't got anything against traditional songs, they're great! But many adults dislike the newer, livelier songs. Most teenagers prefer these songs, we feel more able to worship God and praise him by singing these songs. Let's relax a little, take it easy, accept change, and do what we were made to do – worship God.

I'm sure I've said this before, but I'll say it again since its important. At the end of the day it doesn't matter if you can or can't sing, it doesn't matter whether your hair is green and spiky or neatly plaited, it doesn't matter whether you like drums or prefer a cappella. It doesn't matter whether you're 'happy-clappy' and like waving your hands in the air and dancing, or simply prefer to sit still. What matters, is that you worship God. What matters is whether your worship comes from your heart, and whether you actually mean the words you're singing. At the end of the day, that's all that matters.

Think about it

It's not how you worship, but who you worship, and why you worship. It doesn't matter what style of music you like (just don't criticise other styles), be it loud or quiet; lively, or motionless. What counts is that you worship God from your heart, that you really, truly love him and give him your heartfelt adoration and praise. Just remember, it's all too easy to get carried away in the motions of singing songs and forget who we are singing to.

Prayer

Lord,
    thank you that we can praise and worship you
    in many different ways.
    Help me not to criticise
    the different ways people like to worship you,
    but to be thankful that so many people are worshipping you.
    I know that most young people like noisy, modern songs,
    and that many older people prefer quieter songs;
    help me to remember that you don't mind how I worship.
    Lord, help me to worship you more.
    Amen.

The Uniform of the Church – Dress Regulations

Thou shalt observe the following rules, by order of the vicar:

- As stated in the eleventh commandment, denim is strictly forbidden.
- All women shall wear skirts of regulation length and men shall wear plain ties and dark jackets.
- Trainers are forbidden, as are stilettos (they may damage the floor).
- Shoes should be black and shine well.
- In your right arm you should carry a leather bound Bible, and in your left, money for the collection. (Notes only, please.)
- Metal buttons on clothing are strictly prohibited.

I opened my Bible the other day and looked for the eleventh commandment. It wasn't there, I couldn't find it. I sat and thought for a while and then looked in a concordance. Still no luck, time was running out and I still hadn't found it. Desperate, I dusted down an old commentary and eventually found something about the commandments. It said the commandments were found in Exodus 20. So I looked it up and read them out one at a time. Surprised, I discovered that the last one was missing, there were only ten, 'what's happened to the eleventh? Perhaps I've got a dodgy version,' I thought. I found a different version under a pile of old books in the attic and turned to Exodus 20 once more. Still no luck! I returned to the commentary and read it carefully, it told me that God had given Moses ten commandments, written on tablets of stone.

So what about the eleventh commandment – 'Cast out thy denim'? I asked my vicar that, and he was forced to admit that the Bible doesn't actually say anything of the sort. That's not surprising since denim's a fairly new invention. I asked him, 'What's so evil about denim?' Hard question, he paused, muttered something under his breath and then said that he was sorry we couldn't talk any longer but he had an important meeting to go to. Just like a politician, he always manages to avoid answering the difficult questions!

Young people prefer to dress casually

Perhaps I made up that story, but what does it matter? – the principles are the same. Many people in churches all over the country frown on those who wear jeans. They seem to have made up their own rules that all Christians must follow. But there are only ten commandments, not eleven, nor twelve! These people say it's irreverent to come into God's presence dressed casually. But aren't we in God's presence all day, every day? (After all, God is everywhere!) If I have to dress smartly to go to church, does this mean I can't talk to him when I'm on the loo, or lying in bed wearing my pyjamas? I think it's wrong to say that you must dress smartly to go to church.

The Bible doesn't tell us what we have to wear, it doesn't say we should go to church wearing a suit and tie, or a smart skirt and blouse. Some people want to, and it's not for us to stop them or criticise. But why enforce pointless rules? Few teenagers would want to go to church wearing smart clothes, we feel comfortable wearing denim or other casual clothes. When we are dressed in these clothes we can relax, forget about ourselves and our worries and concentrate on him – the object of our faith.

Paul said that the Gentiles needn't follow all the rules of the Jews. These rules were legalistic and many of them were no longer relevant. He outlined a few simple guidelines which basically said that they should follow Jesus' example, and that's what we should do too.

Sure, business people dress smartly – it creates good impressions with clients. But who are we trying to fool? We can't impress the God of this world, the very God who made the earth, and who made us. Good looks don't make him look upon us more favourably, he knows our motives, he knows our thoughts, he knows us better than we know ourselves!

So why should we have to follow a strict dress code? It's crazy really – we shouldn't have to! As all Sunday school teachers remind us, it's not the outward appearance that matters, but what the heart's like. What counts is where we are in our walk with Jesus. Clothing is just a secondary issue that distracts us from what we should be thinking about – God.

Think about it

Is the way you look when you go to church important? If so, who are you dressing for? Are you dressing for God, or the rest of the Church?

Prayer

Lord Jesus,
  Thank you that I can talk to you wherever I am,
  and that it doesn't matter whether I'm wearing my pyjamas,
  a suit, or holey jeans.
  Help me not to criticise what others wear to church,
  but to remember that what really counts
  is where I am in my walk with you.
  Amen.

Mrs Smith: *All under 21s are brats, that's what I say.*

Mrs C.: *You know, Felicity, we may not have seen eye to eye on things before, but I definitely agree with you on this one. All under 21s are brats, and I should know, I had four of them!*

Mrs Smith: *I'm glad we're in agreement for once.*

Mrs C.: *Huh, kids eh? Who'd have 'em?*

Mrs Smith: *Well, you just said you had four!*

Mrs C.: *That's right. They eat you out of house and home, listen to loud music late at night, spend all your money on designer clothes; and what for? They then expect you to pay for them to go to university.*

Mrs Smith: *Well, as I said, all under 21s are brats.*

Believe it or not, some people actually think like Mrs C. and Mrs Smith! First things first, let's get things straight; it's a myth that all under 21s are brats, in fact most under 21s are fairly polite, and are normal people. So now we know where we're standing, let's try and see why some people think we're nothing more than big noisy kids. From a very young age we've been told time and again that 'You're only young once' – this has been drilled into us. So it's not surprising that we want to make the most of our youth, after all, what's wrong with going to the odd party or listening to good music? Nothing, absolutely nothing!

It's hard to believe, but even old Mrs Smith, and Mrs C. were young once, in fact, every adult was young once. So if you say that all under 21s are brats then you're saying that for the first twenty-one years of your life, you were a brat as well. Not many people would say that kind of thing about themselves! I mean, twenty-one years is a long, long time. In fact, twenty-one years is somewhere between a third and a quarter of the average person's lifetime. There is one other thing I'd like to ask Mrs Smith – does she expect people to go to sleep as 'brats' on the eve of their twenty-first birthday and wake up as mature adults the next morning? Growing up takes time, it doesn't just happen overnight!

If you're not a teenager, try and think back to when you were one and ask yourself if you really were a brat. No, of course you weren't! You probably spent up to forty hours a week studying, so that by the time you'd finished, you'd want to go out and enjoy yourself a bit! That's not so bad, is it? After all, all work and no play never did anyone any good!

It's not just young people who like to have fun!

It may seem odd, but I think we never really grow up, we're all like children in some ways. Even at eighty or ninety, there are still so many experiences we've never had, so many things still to learn that we can still be like children at times. If our bodies could cope with it, we could spend a thousand years or more on the earth and there would still be new things to learn each day. Hopefully, the older we get the more mature we become, and the cleverer we get as we learn more and more things each day. However, it really isn't that simple, some people who are thirty or forty act more like teenagers than some fourteen year-olds do! Even so, most people like to have fun and laugh now and again.

I guess that some adults don't like teenagers simply because we're not always as mature as they are. Fair enough, I can understand that. But if they're really as mature as they think they are, then why don't they help us to understand the world we live in better and to know how we are expected to behave, so that we can become more mature! Instead, what do they do? They criticise us and declare their undying hate of us – a very mature attitude? Well, thanks for your confidence guys. I'm sure my generation will remember it when we're running the country in thirty years or so. Oh, and won't our taxes be used to pay your pensions then!?

Young people can be sensible and committed

On a more serious note, though we do have our short comings, that does not mean that we are hopeless. If you're an adult, I bet your parents said similar things about you when you were young! We do have our uses, in fact I'm surprised that so few adults have recognised these and exploited them! We are young and active, fit, and not easily tired, and . . . wait for it, sensible and committed.

Young people are valuable

Even though we are often criticised, many teenagers are committed Christians and have a valuable role to play in the Church. Teenagers help in the Church in all sorts of ways. We do the gardening, help make the tea and coffee (and if you're nice to us we'll give away free biscuits as well!), plus, we're always eager to help take the offering! We're valuable, we help in all sorts of ways. Some teenagers also play their instruments in the church band, others help out in Sunday school, or even preach.

Think about it

We're not aliens, we're just trying to adjust to the weird and wonderful ways of this world. So please don't prejudge us, give us a chance, treat us like adults and you'll be surprised.

Prayer

Lord Jesus,
    help me to remember that you created humans
    – and that includes teenagers –
    in your own image.
    Help me to appreciate that every teenager
    does have a role to play in the Church.
    Amen.

OH **NO**! NOT ANOTHER **BORING** SERMON ...

Jonathan: ('average' teenager)	Man, you don't really expect me to believe all that church stuff – who does?
Steven: (Christian teenager)	Look Jon, all I'm saying is that church is not like you think it is.
Jonathan:	Sure, and I'm the Prime Minister! Come on dude, get wise, who wants to go to church these days? I mean, talk about boredom. Old ladies sitting on creaky wooden pews smartly wearing gloves, singing out of time to some ancient organ. And if that's not enough, there's some dull guy who calls himself a vicar who thinks he has the right to tell everyone they're livin' in sin. If that doesn't send you to sleep, then wait till the vicar bloke starts talking; you're bound to fall asleep then! Come on mate, wake up to the truth, the Church is not for the teenagers of today!

Steven:	*Since when have you been an expert on religion, Jon? Have you ever actually been to church?*
Jonathan:	*Who says you have to go there to know about it? Besides, as it happens, I have been once, I went to a cousin's wedding in the south of Italy four or five years ago.*
Steven:	*Well mate, I've got a surprise for you, church is nothing like the dull place you just described. It's lively and interesting, even better than that, the message of the Bible is the message of the TRUTH and it is still totally relevant today. Why don't you come along with me and see for yourself? I bet you won't see an organ, and you certainly won't see creaky wooden pews, we have nice comfy chairs at our church.*

If you think the teenage years are confusing, you're not alone, in fact you're probably in the majority. So if you're not a teenager, try remembering what it was like to be one, and if you are one just relax in the knowledge that you're not completely mad, just going through a very crazy time. The term 'teenager' covers an incredibly large cross-section of society, and in so doing, encompasses a huge range of attitudes, ideas, expectations, aims, thoughts, experiences, levels of maturity, styles of handwriting and hair colours. So it's hardly surprising that everyone thinks differently. I may be eighteen, but I am still classed as a teenager, along with a thirteen-year-old, and that's pretty daft, isn't it? I know older teenagers are supposed to be more mature, but that doesn't really matter – sometimes they are and sometimes they aren't! This whole period of life is confusing and can drive you nuts, so when it comes to the Church things are just as insane. Don't expect too much, I'm not promising any easy answers. I'm not going to give you a formula where all you have to do is substitute in the values.

People say that just because someone is older they ought to be more mature. But age hasn't always got much to do with it. Some teenagers are young but really mature and the opposite is also true. It's really no wonder that everyone is so confused. Everyone has different reasons for going to church, there are no simple generalisations to make because of age, gender, or anything else for that matter. Some people go because of friends, some go because they enjoy it, others go because they want to learn more about God, worship him, and have fellowship with other Christians. Motives are important, but what's more important is the fact that so many teenagers do go. I think we should thank God for that and with his help try to give teenagers a warm welcome and make them feel wanted. Let us also pray that God will work in the lives of all the teenagers who go, whatever their motives.

Just forty winks?

Think back, if you can, to that Sunday morning when you let your eyes close for just a second, thinking to yourself all along that you would continue listening to the sermon, but with your eyes closed. I imagine most people can remember a time when that happened. You'd probably had a long, hard, stressful week and an equally lively Saturday, so that when the alarm went off at nine on Sunday morning all you wanted to do was hit it and tell it to shut up. Anyway, after a struggle with your conscience you probably managed to pull up in the church car park a minute or two late, only to look in the rear view mirror and find your hair had gone wild. Feeling flustered you eventually came out of the toilets, and had to walk right to the front in the middle of a quiet moment, feeling sure that everyone was staring at you, watching your face turn red!

At some time in our lives all of us must have experienced a situation like this – whilst the preacher is in the closing 85 minutes of his sermon, your eye lids start to close and you kid yourself that no one will notice and you can still listen with your eyes shut. Of course, it's not until the number of the final hymn has been announced that you realise you have just had an extended forty winks. So with artificial vigour you get up and loudly begin singing 'Morning has broken . . .' only to discover the rest of the congregation is singing a different hymn!

Most of us have probably experienced something like this at some stage in our lives, and embarrassing though it is at the time, manage to look back upon it with a smile! Now and again everyone is unfortunate enough to have to sit through a monotonous sermon that seems to last for most of eternity. Teenagers aren't alone in finding some sermons boring. Besides, it's a well-known fact that most people can only concentrate for about twenty minutes at a time. So unless the preacher wants to have a couple of commercial breaks part way through his sermon and offer a good supply of real chocolate biscuits and strong coffee, it would be better if the sermon remained short!

There's nothing wrong with an interesting sermon!

The purpose of a sermon is to preach the word of God. So why do so many people use methods from centuries ago. A few people have managed to work out how to use OHPs but the majority stick to talking alone. Why not be radical and spice up the odd sermon? Apart from being more interesting, it will probably be listened to much more carefully, so the message is more likely to be applied. Isn't that what's wanted anyway? Technology seems to be advancing quicker than ever before, so why not make use of it on Sundays?

The occasional use of multimedia would be great, a video wall perhaps, or if that's too adventurous, how about a colourful OHP slide? The sky's the limit, let your imagination run wild. How about borrowing a camcorder and conducting some street interviews and playing them back during the service? Alternatively, how about playing a track from a Christian CD? It will be unusual and guaranteed to grab attention, it could also be used as an introduction to the sermon. Why not get a few people together to do something different? How about decorating the building thematically for a week, or if that's too ambitious, simply put on a little sketch that illustrates the passage to be looked at – it will help in visualising it and will probably be quite fun too!

Everyone has their own view of the Church, but most of these views are out of date. If you only go to church for weddings and funerals you'll have no idea what Church is really about. At the beginning of this chapter Jonathan said what he thought of

Church. He was wrong, Church isn't like that anymore, but lots of people think it is. Even though the Church has changed, the message of the gospel hasn't.

Lots of teenagers are leaving the Church today, lots more than ever before. I don't know why, and I'm not sure that anyone does. But something needs to be done, the leaders of tomorrow's Church are the teenagers of today. Perhaps it's because the Church no longer seems relevant to the teenagers of today. Does this mean the Church needs to change? Maybe it does, I'm not sure though. Modern music and jeans might make a difference – but the problems could be much bigger than we realise. We need to think and pray about it.

Think about it

It's not only young people who like interesting sermons – older people do too.

Prayer

Lord,
  help me to make my Sunday school lesson/sermon/talk more interesting.
  It makes sense, because if people are interested they'll listen more,
  and if they listen more they'll learn more about you
  – which is surely the aim.
  Amen.

ALL RIGHT?
HOW IS IT GOING THEN?

Local Councillor: *Ladies and gentlemen, as your local council representative and Chair of this committee, I would like to welcome you to the first 'Youth Strategy and Initiative' meeting in this borough. I hope that we will successfully work together as we share our experiences and ideas. In this meeting, it has been agreed that we will look at the various methods of approaching teenagers, as this will be vital to all our future discussions. Before we begin, perhaps everyone would introduce themselves. Pastor, you first.*

Pastor: *I am the pastor of the local church, and have been asked to act as secretary to this group. I am a parent of two teenagers and also have had much experience with the teenagers in my church.*

Youth Leader:	*Hi everyone, my name's Sandra and I work as a part-time Youth Leader at my local church.*
Head teacher:	*Good evening. I am the head teacher of the local secondary school. I have spent the last thirty-four years in education and so have had extensive experience of teenagers.*
Social worker:	*Hello, I am a social worker and work with youths who have problems.* [To Local Councillor] *May I say a word or two about how I think youths should be approached?* [He nods] *Good. I think that this is a simple issue. I believe you should simply speak to them all in the same way. Simply treat them as kids, after all that's what they are, just big kids. But twice as noisy, and even more difficult to handle!*
Head teacher:	*Certainly not. Though the younger ones may act like kids, the older teenagers, at least, should be treated as adults.*
Local Councillor:	*It's great that we've got a healthy debate going. Perhaps we should listen to the expert – a teenager himself.* [Turns to Youth Leader] *Sandra?*
Youth Leader:	*I asked a teenager, a lad called Phil Portson, to write down how he thought teenagers should be approached. Here it is, there's a copy for everyone.*

Well guys, it's great that you want to hear what I've got to say, but I may as well be frank! If you've come expecting an easy solution or a formula, then forget it. You might as well just go home. So, if you're still eager to hear what I've got to say, then here goes!

Teenagers are humans

Prepare yourselves for some shocking news, teenagers are humans! We are not aliens, we should be treated like everybody else. The teenage years are the most difficult, the hardest, the most complex. Almost overnight, we are expected to be adults, but we are not told how. You must forgive us if we make mistakes. At twelve and a half, we're mere children, but six months later and we've been thrown into a life-changing period. And it's not just life changing for us – it's just as bad for our parents and teachers! Our bodies change shape, we're expected to behave, school work suddenly becomes hard . . . and then, worse still, we're supposed to choose what to study, whether to go to uni, and many other things as well! It's like this, after thirteen quiet years, learning to walk and talk, read and write, and play, play, play; life throws its hardest challenges at us – all at once, too! It's a nightmare, man!

So bear with us, we're not perfect yet! The trouble is, we're all different. And to make matters worse, we have our own slang words that adults don't understand. So what do you say if you meet a teenager in the street, or worse still, sit next to one of us at church on Sunday. Don't be scared; as the old proverb goes, 'the bark's worse than the bite!' For starters, remember this: no one likes to be looked down on. Don't speak with one syllable words, and don't act as if you're superior. You probably are, after all you'll have had years more experience in life, you'll probably be cleverer and you're bound to be richer! Just please don't treat teenagers as if we're inferior, even if you think we are.

Treat us as equals, please!

I think the key to it all is quite simple really; treat us as if we're equals. The hard bit is that you've got to believe that we are equals, before you can start acting that way. You can't pretend that we're equals while not believing it. Teenagers aren't thick – we'll see through your act – and then it'll be worse for you!

Be normal

I think the best thing to do, is to be normal. No pretence, no acting, no awkwardness, no silly jokes, none of that 'I'm Mr Intellectual' stuff. Just be yourself. If you normally talk using really long complicated words, try talking as most people do – normally. Don't suddenly say that everything is wicked or sad, and don't come up to me and tell me that I'm a cool dude! If you do, I won't believe you, that kind of language doesn't sound right if it comes from someone who normally speaks perfectly, and pronounces their ps and qs just so. Treat us as equals, but don't change the way you talk so that it sounds stupid. We do understand the English language, and can actually speak it quite well, when we want!

We may have some 'in' words, but imagine how stupid you'd look if you started using them! 'Hey dude, wasn't that sermon just rad! The preacher geezer's got some cool yellow shoe laces, d'y notice?' Now imagine that coming from someone dressed smartly and who normally talks . . . well, poshly! It sounds ridiculous!

It sounds simple, but it's not. Be normal, and treat us as equals, that's how to approach a teenager – Phil.

Think about it

Are you the social worker or the head teacher? If you're an adult, how do you approach teenagers? Do you think they're just big kids, or do you treat them as equals? Do you speak to teenagers because you feel you have to, or because you want to? Don't worry if you've made some mistakes along the way – everyone has – it's where you go from here that counts.

Prayer

Lord Jesus,
    we have all made mistakes in the past
    and probably will do so again in the future.
    However, because of what you have done for us
    we can ask for forgiveness and help.
    We can approach each new day (and each new teenager)
    with renewed vigour and encouragement.
    Thank you.
    Amen.

... AND OTHER ANNOYING THINGS

Things are just not like they used to be. In my day . . .

Children were seen and not heard.
It was safe for women to go out at night.
Everyone dressed smartly to go to church.
Loud music was forbidden.
Teenagers spoke properly, there were no slang words then.
Sports were not dangerous.
People didn't swear.
Sundays were kept sacred – no leisure activities were allowed.

Sounds familiar, doesn't it? We've all heard these kind of things before and probably will do again. The trouble is, many adults don't even realise they can be annoying. And if they do, then they don't seem to know how to stop it!

Young people don't like to be patronised

Most teenagers are fairly easy going. We can take the odd annoying thing. But what really gets on our nerves is being patronised. It's all too easy to do it, almost without thinking, but it's a real problem. Patronise someone just once, and they might dislike you for years – though you might think that's not so bad sometimes!

Being patronised is irritating, most of us should know, as it happens to almost everyone now and again. It makes you feel like you're not valued, like you're second best. It's almost as if you're being told that it'd have been better if you'd been born fifty years ago, or as if you might as well give up. Whatever the situation, being patronised, or patronising someone else, is just not good enough. So why not stop patronising and be friendly instead? How about listening to other people's views – who knows, maybe you're not as perfect as you thought – maybe you are wrong once in a while!

Sorry folks, but sooner or later someone's got to say what annoys teenagers, and it might as well be sooner! But don't feel got at, I'm not nagging, I'm just trying to make adults more aware of what teenagers don't like.

Young people want to be listened to

Imagine you've just found a solution to the world's second greatest problem (whatever you think that might be). What would you do? You'd tell the world. Phone the PM, call a press conference. You'd tell anyone who'd listen. But wouldn't it be awful if no one would listen, if you were ignored. Time would pass. You'd be itching to hand out your solution but no one would listen. And suddenly, the disaster arrives, it passes and as you predicted, a dreadful thing happened. The trouble is, even though people will listen to you now, it's too late!

It's like this in a way with teenagers. We haven't solved all the world's problems (not yet, anyway!), but we do have valuable views and opinions. We can see the world differently from adults, we look at things in a different way. It's all too easy for us to be ignored, and that is really frustrating. To know that you've got something valuable to say, but no one listens, is really annoying. Please don't ignore us, we're not just big kids, we're not just second best! But the fact that you're reading this means you do care, it means that you are listening to teenagers already, and that's really great!

Young people want to be taken seriously

You know, some adults think we're nothing more than big kids. Admittedly there are loads of teenagers who are thirteen or fourteen, who are nothing more than big kids, but even then, many of them are sensible. But what about the rest of us? The fifteen, sixteen, seventeen year-olds and so on. Even some of the thirteen and fourteen year-olds aren't big kids. Please be fair and give us a chance. One thing that is really annoying is being treated as kids. Treat us as we behave, that's fair, isn't it? That means many of us should be treated like adults – in other words, treat us as equals.

Young people don't like to be taken for granted

One thing that many people seem to forget is that teenagers aren't slaves or servants. I'm often happy to help but I hate to be taken for granted. It's all too easy to take a teenager for granted, to expect a teenager to do something. The odd 'thank you' now and again doesn't hurt anyone! We're not perfect yet, but be patient with us and show your appreciation. The old saying 'Please be patient God hasn't finished working on me yet' is so appropriate. We're very imperfect, but we're still humans, so please don't take us for granted.

After so many things that annoy us, you might wonder if there's anything we like or find pleasing. In fact, I think that most things are not annoying and I generally enjoy life! Thanks and encouragement, help and lots of other things are all pleasing. Basically it's the opposite of all that I've said annoys us! It's that simple!

If there's a negative, there's probably a positive as well, there is in this case, anyhow. Every time you go to take a teenager for granted, criticise or do any of the other really annoying things, think again. Wouldn't it be great if you could be nice instead. Be positive, say a word of encouragement or praise. Show some respect, or lend a listening ear. Be radical and treat us as equals even when others don't. Remember that we can see things differently, so talk to us, ask us our views, show you care, or are interested.

Think about it

We may not be the greatest, or the cleverest, but we are human! And as humans we do deserve to be listened to, appreciated and treated well. I can't speak for all young people, but I know if I'm treated well I return the favour and treat that person extra nicely, so it's worth it in the end! So what about it? Give it a try and see what happens.

Prayer

Lord Jesus,
    help me to remember that teenagers are humans also.
    Help me to give them a chance and treat them well.
    Amen.

08:00 Alarm clock goes off

08:10 Crawl out of bed, wash and dress

08:25 Breakfast

08:30 Leave for school

08:43 Arrive, breathless

08:45 School begins

09:05 First lesson – Maths (Not awake enough to concentrate!)

10:05 Second lesson – Maths (Again)

11:05 Break. Time to eat!

11:25 Third lesson – Physics

12:25 Fourth lesson – English

13:25 Lunch. Visit the local chip shop!

14:05 Afternoon registration

14:15 Last lesson – History

15:15 School ends. Go home. Relax

16:00 Start homework

17:30 Tea (or dinner, if you're lucky!)

18:30 Continue homework (and revision)

21:00 onwards. More homework/time to go out/watch
TV/do other things/think about going to bed!

That, my friends, is the hectic life of Mr Teenager. Of course, it does change from day to day. He may go to work some evenings (if he's sixteen or older), or he might just go out with some friends or go to a church youth group. But to tell the truth, every teenager is different, and every day for every teenager is different! But the average day for the average teenager might be something like the one described above. But then again, it might not!

You might be wondering what's so special about the life of a teenager? What's different about the lifestyle of a teenager from adults and children? And what about Christian teenagers and non-Christian ones? Well, read on for my ideas and see if you agree.

Anyone who is a teenager, or has been one, knows a bit about the teenage years being some of the hardest. Because of this, our lives are often different from adults and children. We have lots of homework and sometimes have to spend many hours doing it – what a bore! We like to go out, to enjoy ourselves, to have fun. As we grow older we somehow discover a greater sense of freedom and we come to be more independent, bit by bit.

We like to do things by ourselves more and sometimes experiment with things. That's when things can go wrong or get out of hand. Teenagers want to learn lots of new things about the world around us, but this can be dangerous sometimes.

There are, or at least should be, many differences between Christian teenagers and non-Christian ones. For many teenagers, there are so many unusual and wonderful things to be discovered. The trouble is, there are also lots of bad things that many teenagers find out, like getting drunk, smoking, or trying drugs. Even some teenagers who go to church experiment with all these crazy things. The Church needs to do more here, to help the teenagers of today deal with all the crazy problems that are thrown at us. Christian teenagers often live very different lives from non-Christian ones. This is for all sorts of reasons, often because many of us do not go and get drunk, take drugs, or sleep around. Things go deeper than this as well. Our very title as 'Christians' means that we will get teased and tormented.

Young people find it hard to be Christians at school

Perhaps a bit of persecution shouldn't matter when we'll get to spend all of our lives with our Saviour one day, but it does. It can be hard to cope with and it's not nice being rejected, or bullied because of what you believe in. Also, it's our job as Christians to live the way Jesus wants us to, in our schools and places of work. And that doesn't make it any easier – in fact, it makes it a whole lot harder! Today most people reject Christianity without ever thinking about it or considering the evidence, they don't believe there is a God. This makes it even harder for Christians to survive at school, and harder still to witness.

As Christians our lives are different, our lifestyles are different. Many Christian young people don't smoke, don't swear, don't mis-use God's name and don't sleep around. We're not super moral people, we're just normal guys, but we are trying to live the way Jesus wants us to, and with his help, that should make a big difference!

And at least some of the time, it does. If we are really living as true Christians, people notice the difference. They want to know why we're different. This is often a great time to tell friends and others bits about our faith. This is also when bullying, persecution and tormenting can happen. Some teenagers, especially those who are firm in their faith, can cope with this but others find it really hard. But no matter who you are, it's still not easy.

But we need to use these opportunities to tell our peers about why we believe in God. Perhaps we can invite them along to CU (Christian Union) or to a church Youth Group. But whatever we do, we can be a living example, showing them what a real Christian is.

Think about it

Teenagers do have different lifestyles from others. The way all Christians live their lives really does matter, for our lives can be a living witness to the wonderful saving power of Jesus Christ.

So, are you living right? Is your lifestyle like Jesus'?

Prayer

Lord Jesus,
   when it comes down to it,
   I know I need to make you my role model,
   to be more like you in every way.
   Help me to do this.
   Amen.

Picture the scene: at a youth camp somewhere down south, there are about one hundred teenagers and another twenty leaders sitting in a large marquee. It's late at night and someone is reading out a list of notices for the next day.

Leader: *I have one more notice, and then you're free to go and get your hot chocolate. Tomorrow afternoon's optional seminar will be on . . .*

Pause.

Leader: *It.*

Puzzled silence. *(I wondered, does he mean what I think he does?)*

13-year old girl: [Shouts] *Sex!*

Leader: *Yes, we are going to be talking about . . . 'It'. We shall start at half past two and will be in the main tent – make sure you're there!*

Let's talk about sex

It's a sad state of affairs when we can't say the word 'sex', but have to use 'it' instead. Sorry folks, but this really did happen. At a youth camp I was on a few years back, one of the leaders really did call sex, 'it'. Admittedly, it had been a long day, so perhaps the leader was trying to see if anyone was listening, (and not many people were!) but I think the mention of chocolate might have woken everyone up anyhow!

It's not as if sex is some new-fangled thing that's only just been discovered – if it had, we wouldn't be here today! Sex is as old as mankind, so why are we scared of talking about it? Why do we have a hundred and one other words for it? Perhaps it's to do with the mystery surrounding it. After all, for the first twelve or thirteen years of our lives we are more or less kept in the dark about our origins.

Think back to when you first learnt about sex. It was probably when you were between ten and thirteen years old. At that age you probably thought you'd got life sussed – you could read and write, you knew most of your times tables and you could ride a bike. What else is there to life? Then suddenly you realise that there's lots you don't know – almost out of the blue, your parents or an embarrassed teacher tell you about how you came into the world. Perhaps it's because we're not taught about sex for so many years, that it seems somehow mysterious, and so lots of other words are used instead of 'sex.' I think we need to talk about sex more, without getting embarrassed about it.

In a sex-crazy society, sex sells

Sex is God's incredible way of allowing us to reproduce. The trouble is, sex has been abused. To many people it is no longer the gift that God intended it to be. Every day, over a thousand teenage girls in America alone have an abortion. Almost as many give birth to babies, even though they are not married and in most cases aren't able to look after the baby properly. If you think that's bad, then what about this? Every day in America over four thousand teenagers catch a sexually transmitted disease. Worse still, around eighty teenagers are raped every day. I think we're living in a sex-mad society.

That's not the whole story either. Sex has got out of hand in a big way. Take the media for example, sex sells. Put 'sex' on the cover of your magazine or paper and you can bet loads of people will buy it. Or just watch the news, almost everyday we hear of people committing sex-related crimes. I say it again, I think we're in a sex-crazy society. I even read somewhere that the average male thinks about sex once every ten seconds.

So what can we do? Things can get worse, and they probably will if we don't do something to stop it. The youth leader who I talked about at the start of this chapter has already done something. Though I didn't like him calling sex, 'it', he was at least prepared to talk about sex. He was even holding a seminar on sex, and that's not so bad. At that seminar he did talk about sex, he talked about sex and marriage, what's right and what's not, and a whole lot more as well. That's what needs to happen today, we need to talk about it. It's all too easy to keep sex a secret, to not talk about it. We need to change that, to bring it into the open and discuss it.

Many non-Christian teenagers today think the Church's views on sex are outdated. They think the Church is still in Victorian times where sex is concerned. They don't understand why Christians believe that sex should be kept for marriage. The average teenager of today believes there's nothing wrong with sleeping around. In fact, far too many do sleep around freely. There is a huge gap between what Christian teenagers believe and what the average teenager of today believes. We need to think and pray about what we're going to do; there is no easy solution, but with God's help we can make a difference.

Tempted to sin

The devil knows better than most about Christian young people and sex. He knows when young people are vulnerable, and he gets us when we're down, trying to tempt us and persuade us that it's all right to sin – just the once. But one can soon become two and then three and four. However, it's not all right to sin. Just because I'm a Christian doesn't make it any easier, life doesn't suddenly become perfect. The temptations are still there and they seem to get worse by the day. Besides, it's all too easy to make up excuses for our actions at the time and then have regrets later. There is no easy way out, we have to struggle at times. Sexual sin can be very tempting, but must be resisted. It would be really great if Christian adults could pray for the teenagers they know. This is often the kind of thing teenagers prefer not to talk about – and that's fair enough – but if adults prayed for the young people they know, then who knows what might happen? God can do amazing things when Christians get down on their knees and pray.

Think about it

We're supposed to be in the world but not a part of the world – but that's easier said than done! We need to pray for each other, that we may be salt and light. Do you pray for the young people you know? They're probably finding it hard and would really value your prayers.

'Resist the devil, and he will flee from you.' James 4:7b (NIV)

Prayer

Lord,
    when things get hard,
    when I'm tempted to sin,
    help me to resist the devil.
    I know it's not easy
    – it never is –
    but teenagers can find it just as hard,
    if not harder.
    I just pray that you will help the young people I know
    to resist the devil also,
    and find the strength to win through.
    Amen.

I'LL HUFF, AND I'LL PUFF, AND I'LL ...

Behind the bike shed on a wintry November afternoon, three lads sit huddled together, talking and smoking. They're all about thirteen or fourteen years of age.

Pete: *Here you are Ju, try one of these.*

Ju: *Thanks, but all the same I'd better not. My mum'd kill me if she ever found out!*

Dan: *Yeah, and she'd kill you if she knew you were skiving maths.*

Pause

Ju: *Don't remind me! Huh, you should hear what she thinks about ciggies.*

Pete: *I'd rather not!*

Ju:	*'They cause yer cancer and they cost yer money, an' if that's not enough yer nails turn yeller and yer get a nasty cough.'*
Pete:	*Nah, you don't wanna listen to that rubbish, I'm still captain of the school football team and I've been smoking for ages. You see, it's made me fitter if anything.*
Dan:	*Smoking or not, how many games have you won in the last season?*
Pete:	*Shut up you! Just 'cause you wasn't picked for the team.*
Dan:	*If I had been, we might have won at least one of the last ten games!*
Ju:	*Stop it you two. I'm freezing!*
Dan:	*Well have a fag, it'll warm you up no end.*
Ju:	*Oh, I dunno.*
Pete:	*Here you are, I'll light it for you.*
Dan:	*Go on, it's not like Pete to give away fags.*
Ju:	*Oh, I suppose so, just the once though.*

Young people need to know the facts

Everyday four hundred and fifty children, like Ju, start smoking. Tragically many of them do not realise the dangers of smoking and how hazardous it is. Even though most schools spend many hours teaching about smoking and drugs, children and teenagers often do not believe it. Dying of cancer fifty years after you start smoking is not much of a big deterrent. And anyway, everyone's heard of an Uncle Alf who lived to ninety-nine by smoking sixty a day and having a fry-up for breakfast every morning. At the age of ten, or twelve, or fifteen, it's all too easy to believe that we can live how we want and it won't affect us later on in life – just look at how much chocolate the average teenager eats!

How about putting it this way instead? Take one thousand children from Britain who start smoking. Of those one thousand children, one will be murdered. Now there's not a lot the average person can do to prevent that, apart from using common sense. But six of those children will die in a car crash sometime in their lives. We have done lots to try to reduce that number, we should wear seat belts; plus, lots of other car safety systems have been invented. However, a staggering five hundred of those one thousand children will die of smoking-related diseases. The odds of dying from smoking related diseases seem to be pretty high. I wonder, do the young people know these stunning facts when they start smoking?

The problem is similar with drugs. Everyday many teenagers try drugs and some of them get addicted. There are lots of different drugs and they all have different effects, but no one can disagree that most of them are very dangerous and potentially lethal. All it takes is a bit of peer pressure and another young person's started taking drugs. Soft drugs can lead to hard drugs, which can lead to anything – other crimes to fund the habit, or even death. There are all sorts of reasons why teenagers take drugs and I can't even guess half of them. Some do it because of peer pressure, they do it to become one of the gang, to be liked by friends. Some teenagers do it because they need to escape, they think it is a way out. And I suppose that in the short term, it is a way out. Drugs may help you to forget your problems for a few hours while you're on a very dangerous trip. A trip that might cost you your life.

Prevention, cure, or both?

We all know that prevention is better than cure, but in this day and age I think we need both. One way to try and prevent teenagers from taking drugs in the first place is peer education. This means some teenagers tell others about drugs and their dangers. It doesn't mean someone stands in front of a class of bored teenagers for an hour telling them a bunch of silly stories. It's about the plain facts, telling the teenagers the plain facts in a way they are likely to remember. I had a go at this, and I think it does have an effect. For some reason, they are more likely to listen to people their own age, than to the teachers who give them detentions and set them hours of homework most nights.

Tempted?

The temptations to smoke, drink absurd amounts of alcohol or take drugs are very real. Teenagers do face these temptations; most win through, but some don't. All these things are very dangerous and may even be lethal. All young people need to be prepared for such temptations, but when they come from friends or people you respect this can be extra hard; the old cliché still gives the best advice, 'Just say no.'

There are so many experiences to be had in life, so many things to see and do that we'll never have time for all of them. There are also many experiences that many of us don't ever want to have! It's all too easy to get started on a pathway to misery and boredom, a pathway that eventually leads to death. Addictions to gambling, drinking alcohol, smoking and taking drugs are just some of the things that are so easy to start doing but can be so hard to stop. Every day, so many teenagers begin a habit that is literally a passport to doom, a one-way ticket to destruction.

Think about it

Wasn't Jesus friends with the outcasts of society, the very people who were despised and hated? He was. And I guess that means we should be too. Let's aim to make a difference, to help addicts to quit, to teach others not to start; and to show everyone the narrow path to heaven, not the motorway to hell.

Prayer

Lord,
    help me to care even for those I'd rather avoid;
    to be a good Samaritan and stop to help,
    and not walk past on the other side of the road.
    Amen.

THIS HOUSE BELIEVES THAT ALL PARENTS SHOULD BUY THEIR TEENAGERS DESIGNER TRAINERS.

Proposing the motion: Janice Stock [JS]
Opposing the motion: Frederick Ballwood [FB]

JS: *Good evening ladies and gentlemen. No one can disagree that we should give our children a good start in life. No parent would want their son or daughter to be laughed at because of the clothes they wear. So why do so many parents say 'no' to named products? They may be expensive but I believe that it's a good investment. It's an investment in the life of your child.*

FB: *Alright guys? Now I'm cool, because I'm me. I'm an individual, I'm not like anyone else. Anyone with real street cred is someone who is themselves. It's silly to try and be one of the crowd, to try and fit in and be someone or something that you are not.*

JS: *Wait a moment, you're getting carried away! The issue at hand is whether or not we should buy our teenagers designer trainers.*

FB: *Exactly, let me finish. I'm saying that designer trainers make us one of the crowd. It's like a uniform, everyone wears the same thing, the same make, the same name.*

JS: *No. Now you're being silly, there are lots of different styles and makes.*

FB: *Maybe, but they're still the designer brand, the known name that lots of others have. But not everyone can afford designer trainers, they're a luxury. Besides, why should some children try and force others to buy these trainers? I think the real issue is peer pressure. It's about some teenagers telling others what they have to wear and what they should say and do. It's about one teenager dictating what another teenager's parents should buy for their son or daughter.*

JS: *There's nothing wrong with helping your son or daughter to have some street cred and to look good in the eyes of their mates. Besides, everyone knows designer trainers are better for your feet.*

FB: *Sorry, I disagree. When it comes down to peer pressure, there's a lot wrong with it.*

What is peer pressure?

So what is peer pressure? It's a word we're always hearing, but not quite understanding. It seems to have become the catch phrase of the 90s. It's something every parent's heard and is wary of but no one's really sure why.

Well, here's my definition. It's probably different from the one you'd find in a dictionary or encyclopaedia but here goes anyway! Peer pressure is simply the pressure that teenagers feel from their peers, their friends, people their own age. This pressure is something that makes them want to fit in, it makes them want to be like their friends.

The trouble with peer pressure is that it can make teenagers (and children) do wrong things. It's all too easy to say that peer pressure is harmless but it's not. It's not just about the clothes we wear and how our hair looks, it can get a lot worse. Peer pressure can make teenagers smoke or steal.

Let me tell you about Bill. Bill was your average sort of teenager and for all his life he'd lived in the small village of Highfield. At Highfield he'd always been popular. Everyone had heard of Bill, he was good at Maths, Science and English, but not only that, he could draw and was even good at sports. In fact, he was excellent at sports. Half of the trophies in the school's trophy cabinet had been won by him, for swimming, running, football and basketball. Just when Bill was preparing to race in the school's biggest run – which he hoped to win – his dad came home with some awful news. His dad told him that he'd been offered a new job and they would be moving to a big city a long way away.

Just after his fourteenth birthday, the day before the big race, Bill and his parents moved house. Bill had all of the summer holidays to amuse himself as he had no friends in the big city. Bill was lonely all by himself with no one to play with or talk to. So when the time came for Bill to start school, he decided that he wanted to make lots of friends so he wouldn't be lonely anymore.

Bill's friends were popular, everyone liked them and everyone wanted to be one of them. Bill was proud that they'd chosen him to be one of their group, so he wanted to please them. Bill was worried they'd go off him once they realised he was boring. So he tried to become like them, he started swearing so he could impress them. Then one day, one of his friends offered him a cigarette, this friend told him that if he didn't have it they'd stop being friends. Bill didn't want to lose his only friends, so he had to have it. It wasn't long before Bill started drinking and taking drugs as well. He didn't want to do these things but he knew that if he didn't look 'hard', his friends would stop liking him.

Peer pressure is dangerous

What happened to Bill could happen to anyone. He did these things because he wanted to be seen as being 'cool' and 'hard'. He wanted to be with the 'in' crowd and would do anything for them. There are lots of Bills in this world, lots of teenagers who feel insecure and want to belong to the popular group. It's all too easy for 'normal' teenagers to become like Bill, almost overnight. It's often the Bills of this world who go around smoking and taking drugs. Bill's reason was that he was insecure, he wanted friends so he did what they said. It's not just the Bills of this world who smoke and take drugs but others too. The reasons are often very personal and very individual, but many of them do it because of peer pressure, because they want to be one of a group.

If peer pressure is so dangerous, and I think it is, then more needs to be done about it. I think the Church as a whole, and more especially, youth leaders, need to be more aware of it. But it's no good just knowing about it, action is needed as well. It's not easy to know what can be done as every person's circumstances are different. But it's clear that teenagers need to be educated about peer pressure, they need to know the difficulties they might face before they happen. In my experience schools do teach about peer pressure but possibly this isn't enough. Being a teenager is hard enough, but being a teenager and a Christian is doubly hard. Perhaps the Church could educate Christian teenagers that extra bit more about peer pressure.

It's not just the youth leaders and the pastors who can do things, every Church member can do something as well. I know I've said this before, but I'll say it again since it's so important, when Christians pray, things happen. If every adult Christian were to pray for the young people they know, incredible things could happen.

Think about it

No one can deny that peer pressure is real and dangerous. Everyone has a responsibility to pray, so let's think big, pray lots and listen to what God tells us to do, making sure we're ready to act.

Prayer

Lord Jesus,
    as the times change,
    so do the needs of the people around us.
    Peer pressure seems to be a scary issue at the moment
    and it needs to be addressed urgently.
    I pray, Lord, for the young people I know,

asking that you will help them not to give in to temptations
or peer pressure,
but that they will stand strong for you.
Amen.

OH **NO!** NOT SOME **MORE** HOMEWORK,
I'VE ALREADY GOT THREE HOURS' WORTH TO DO TONIGHT.

Youth leader:	*Youth work.*
Elder:	*(Surprised) Do they? First I've heard of it. My wife's a teacher too and she says they don't.*
Youth leader:	*(Laughs) No, probably not. But what I meant, was that we need to talk about the church's youth work; the youth club and Bible study class.*

Did you know that 76.3 per cent of all statistics are made up? Incredible, eh? I've got some good news for you, the next bit of information is in the remaining 23.7 per cent, that is, it's not made up! The average teenager spends twelve and a half thousand hours at school. It's really amazing that so much time is spent at school. In twelve and a half thousand hours, over six thousand football matches could be watched (or played); or at four pounds an hour, fifty thousand pounds could be earned; or, perish the thought, thirty thousand episodes of *Neighbours* could be viewed!

Isn't it crazy then that so much time is spent at school? I don't think so, I think it is a much better investment of time than almost anything else, it's a preparation for life. For it is in this so-called safe environment that we teenagers can develop and mature, being prepared for the big wide world outside.

Most of the time I love school and I think it would be great if more people felt the same way about it. After all, what's the point in wasting twelve and a half thousand hours of your life? I say 'enjoy it, and you'll get more out of it'. Education really is a wonderful thing and most people do come to appreciate it at some stage in their lives. Everyone who is educated has an incredible head start in society, a head start that is guaranteed to help them, if only they bother to take advantage of it.

Young people need to be motivated

Many young people realise that education is a wonderful opportunity, but find it hard to take advantage of it. There is a huge problem which so many people face, it is a lack of motivation. This is tragic but there is no easy remedy to it either, as far as I know. It is all too easy to come home after a long, hard day at school and sit in front of the television or play some sport. It is much harder to sit at a desk and do hours of studying. So it is all the more important that teenagers are encouraged in what they do but not made to feel so intensely pressurised that they feel they've failed if they don't make the mark.

On the whole I think life is great, but in today's world where technology is rapidly advancing, there is so much competition; in retail and business, on the sports track and in the halls of academia. Competition is stronger than ever in education, so things are not likely to be easy for any teenager. But I believe that he who perseveres will eventually win through, and it is important to win through, for we must use the talents and abilities God has given us to the full.

The Church can educate too

The Church also has an opportunity to educate Christian churchgoing teenagers. Every Sunday the Church has about an hour to teach either with a sermon or in a Bible class. The Church only has a fraction of the time that schools have, after all what's one hour a week? Not a lot, but as they say, 'every penny counts,' and one hour a week over a period of, say, ten years is quite a significant amount. Five hundred and twenty hours of valuable input into the lives of teenagers. And if your church has youth activities as well, then the chances are that it educates teenagers for a lot more than one hour a week. Wow! – think what could be achieved in that time. So many teenagers could be successfully taught to live their lives for God in an incredible way. So let's really make sure that the Church does take advantage of the time that it has and make a difference in today's society.

Strange as it may seem, the Church as a whole seems to have very little to do with the education system of today, even though education is such a major player in the lives of so many teenagers. Although the Church has its own opportunities on Sundays to educate some young people, very few go to church, so not many of them ever come into contact with Christian adults. Some individual Christians do go into schools and that's really great. They leave the 'safe' environment of the Church and go out to schools. They go to do all sorts of things, to take assemblies, to give out Bibles, to lead Christian Unions or to teach RE lessons. I think it's wonderful that so many Christians do play a part in the education of teenagers.

Think about it

What role do you, or your Church, play in the education of Christian teenagers? Do you go to schools and teach, lead assemblies or Christian Unions? Or is it your place to support those who do these things? Is there something you could do that would help to make a difference?

Prayer

Lord Jesus,
    thank you that so many millions of children and teenagers
    can benefit from education.
    Should I be playing a bigger role in education,
    perhaps helping at my local school in some way,
    or supporting those that do?
    Amen.